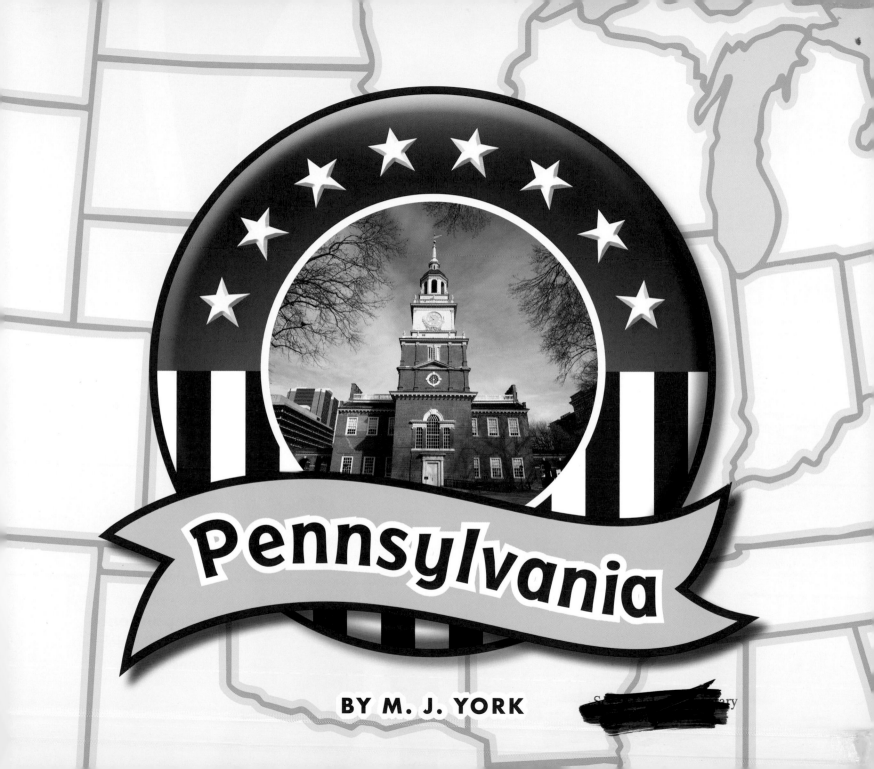

Pennsylvania

BY M. J. YORK

The Child's World

Published by The Child's World®
1980 Lookout Drive • Mankato, MN 56003-1705
800-599-READ • www.childsworld.com

ACKNOWLEDGMENTS
The Child's World®: Mary Berendes, Publishing Director
The Design Lab: Design and production
Red Line Editorial: Editorial direction

PHOTO CREDITS: Big Stock Photo, cover, 1, 3; Matt Kania/Map Hero, Inc., 4,
5; Andrea Gingerich/iStockphoto, 7; Shutterstock Images, 9; iStockphoto, 10,
21; Jill Lang/Shutterstock Images, 11; Cynthia Farmer/Shutterstock Images,
13; North Wind Picture Archives/Photolibrary, 15; Gabe Palmer/Photolibrary,
17; Koji Sasahara/AP Images, 19; One Mile Up, 22; Quarter-dollar coin
image from the United States Mint, 22

LIBRARY OF CONGRESS CATALOGING-IN-PUBLICATION DATA
York, M. J., 1983–
  Pennsylvania / by M.J. York.
     p. cm.
  Includes bibliography and index.
  ISBN 978-1-60253-482-7 (library bound : alk. paper)
  1. Pennsylvania—Juvenile literature. I. Title.

F149.3.Y67 2010
974.8—dc22

                                    2010019321

Printed in the United States of America in Mankato, Minnesota.
July 2010
F11538

On the cover:
Many people visit
Independence
Hall in Philadelphia,
Pennsylvania.

CONTENTS

Geography

Let's explore Pennsylvania! Pennsylvania is in the eastern United States. The northwestern corner of the state is on Lake Erie.

Lake Erie is one of the five Great Lakes. The others are Lake Superior, Lake Michigan, Lake Huron, and Lake Ontario.

CANADA

Lake Erie

NEW YORK

WEST NORTH EAST SOUTH

Erie

OHIO

Allegheny River

Wellsboro

Scranton

Williamsport

Pittston

Punxsutawney

PENNSYLVANIA

Ohio River

Tarentum

Altoona

Allentown

Delaware River

Pittsburgh

Harrisburg

Reading

Hershey

Appalachian Mountains

Lancaster

Philadelphia

Gettysburg

Susquehanna River

NEW JERSEY

MARYLAND

DELAWARE

WEST VIRGINIA

VIRGINIA

Cities

Harrisburg is the capital of Pennsylvania. Philadelphia is the state's largest city. About 1.5 million people live there. Pittsburgh, Erie, and Scranton are other well-known cities.

Philadelphia is located on the Delaware River. ▶

Land

Pennsylvania has many rocky hills. It has deep river valleys. The Appalachian Mountains cut through the middle of the state. Pennsylvania has four major rivers: the Ohio River, the Delaware River, the Allegheny River, and the Susquehanna River.

The Allegheny National Forest is in northwestern Pennsylvania. ▶

Plants and Animals

The state animal of Pennsylvania is the white-tailed deer. The state **game** bird is the ruffed grouse. Both live in the forests. The state flower is the mountain laurel. The pink flower grows during the spring and summer.

The mountain laurel grows on Pennsylvania's ▶ rocky and wooded hills.

People and Work

Almost 12.5 million people live in Pennsylvania. **Manufacturing** is important in the state. People make food, medicine, clothes, and **chemicals**. There are also many coal mines. Some people invent new **technology**.

Eggs, mushrooms, and milk are important farm products in Pennsylvania.

This factory in Nazareth, Pennsylvania, produces cement. ▶

History

People from Europe settled the Pennsylvania area in the 1600s. In the 1750s and 1760s, they fought with each other and with Native Americans in the area. During the **American Revolution**, a group of men met in Philadelphia to talk about forming a new government. Many battles of the American Revolution were fought in the state. Pennsylvania became the second U.S. state on December 12, 1787.

Many battles of the U.S. **Civil War** also took place in Pennsylvania, including the Battle of Gettysburg. ▶

The Battle of Gettysburg was the bloodiest battle of the Civil War.

Ways of Life

A lot of important U.S. history happened in Pennsylvania. Battlefields from the American Revolution and the Civil War are in the state. The Declaration of Independence and the U.S. Constitution were written here. Visitors can see the places where these events happened.

Some people in Pennsylvania act out Civil War battles. ▶

Famous People

U.S. President James Buchanan was born in Pennsylvania. Comedian Bill Cosby is from Pennsylvania, too. Golfer Arnold Palmer and actor Will Smith are also from the state.

The founders of two food companies were from Pennsylvania. H. J. Heinz made Heinz ketchup, and Milton Hershey made Hershey's chocolate.

Will Smith has starred in many movies and has had a career in music, too. ▶

Famous Places

Tourists in Pennsylvania can visit Independence Hall in Philadelphia. The Liberty Bell is also in Philadelphia. Visitors can view the crack in its side. People **hike** through the mountains on the Appalachian Trail. The trail crosses the United States from the north to the south.

The Liberty Bell weighs about 2,000 pounds (907 kg). ▶

State Symbols

Seal

Pennsylvania's state seal has a **shield** with an eagle on top. The eagle stands for the United States. Go to childsworld.com/links for a link to Pennsylvania's state Web site, where you can get a firsthand look at the state seal.

Flag

The center shield on Pennsylvania's state flag is similar to the state seal. It shows a ship, a **plow**, and wheat.

Quarter

Pennsylvania's state quarter shows the statue from the top of the state's capitol building. The shape in the upper-left corner is a **keystone**. Pennsylvania is called "the Keystone State." The quarter came out in 1999.

Glossary

American Revolution (uh-MER-ih-kin rev-uh-LOO-shun): During the American Revolution, from 1775 to 1783, the 13 American colonies fought against Britain for their independence. During the American Revolution, men met in Pennsylvania to talk about forming a new government.

chemicals (KEM-uh-kulz): Chemicals are substances used in chemistry. Some chemicals are made in Pennsylvania.

Civil War (SIV-il WOR): In the United States, the Civil War was a war fought between the Northern and the Southern states from 1861 to 1865. The Battle of Gettysburg was a Civil War battle fought in Pennsylvania.

game (GAYM): Game means an animal that is hunted by humans. The ruffed grouse is Pennsylvania's state game bird.

hike (HYK): To hike is to take a walk in a natural area, such as a hill or a mountain. People in Pennsylvania can hike on the Appalachian Trail.

independence (in-deh-PEN-denss): Independence is freedom. The Declaration of Independence was written in Pennsylvania.

keystone (KEY-stohn): A keystone is the stone at the top of an arch that holds the arch together. A keystone appears on the Pennsylvania state quarter.

manufacturing (man-yuh-FAK-chur-ing): Manufacturing is the task of making items with machines. Many people work in manufacturing in Pennsylvania.

plow (PLAU): A plow is a tool that is used to turn over soil before planting seeds. The plow appears on Pennsylvania's state flag.

seal (SEEL): A seal is a symbol a state uses for government business. Pennsylvania's seal shows items that stand for the United States.

shield (SHEELD): A shield is a symbol or emblem. A shield appears on Pennsylvania's state seal.

symbols (SIM-bulz): Symbols are pictures or things that stand for something else. The seal and the flag are Pennsylvania's symbols.

technology (tek-NAWL-uh-jee): Technology is scientific knowledge applied to practical things. Some workers in Pennsylvania invent new technology.

tourists (TOOR-ists): Tourists are people who visit a place (such as a state or country) for fun. Many tourists come to Pennsylvania to see historical places.

Further Information

Books

Kane, Kristin. *K is for Keystone: A Pennsylvania Alphabet*. Chelsea, MI: Sleeping Bear Press, 2003.

Keller, Laurie. *The Scrambled States of America*. New York: Henry Holt, 2002.

Noble, Trinka Hakes. *One for All: A Pennsylvania Number Book*. Chelsea, MI: Sleeping Bear Press, 2005.

Web Sites

Visit our Web site for links about Pennsylvania: *childsworld.com/links*

Note to Parents, Teachers, and Librarians: We routinely verify our Web links to make sure they are safe and active sites. So encourage your readers to check them out!

Index